INVENTIONS
THAT CHANGED
THE WORLD

ROBERT FULTON
and the STEAMBOAT

Angela Royston

PowerKiDS
press

NEW YORK

Published in 2016 by **The Rosen Publishing Group**
29 East 21st Street, New York, NY 10010

Produced for Rosen by Calcium

Editors for Calcium: Harriet McGregor and Sarah Eason
Designers: Jessica Moon and Paul Myerscough
Picture Research: Harriet McGregor

Picture credits: Cover: Getty Images: PhotoQuest (fg); Shutterstock: Everett Historical (bkgd).
Insides: Dreamstime: Songquan Deng 16, Piet Hagenaars 15, Georgios Kollidas 5, 28, Mtsue
4–5; Library of Congress: Detroit Publishing Company 17, 29; Shutterstock: Everett Historical
9, 18, 22, Andy Lidstone 7, Anatoliy Lukich 27, Ian Scott 19; Wikimedia Commons: 6, 14, 21, 23,
25, 26–27, Ron Cogswell 13, Ji-Elle 11, World Imaging 10.

Cataloging-in-Publication Data
Royston, Angela.
Robert Fulton and the steamboat / by Angela Royston.
p. cm. — (Inventions that changed the world)
Includes index.
ISBN 978-1-5081-4635-3 (pbk.)
ISBN 978-1-5081-4636-0 (6-pack)
ISBN 978-1-5081-4637-7 (library binding)
1. Fulton, Robert, 1765 - 1815 — Juvenile literature. 2. Marine engineers — United States
— Biography — Juvenile literature. 3. Inventors — United States — Biography — Juvenile
literature. 4. Steamboats — United States — History — 19th century — Juvenile literature.
I. Royston, Angela, 1945-. II. Title.
VM140.F9 R69 2016
623.82'4—d23

Manufactured in the United States of America
CPSIA Compliance Information: Batch BW16PK: For Further Information contact Rosen Publishing, New York, New York at 1-800-237-9932

CONTENTS

CHANGING THE WORLD

Robert Fulton changed the world, not by inventing the first steamship, but by setting up the first regular steamboat service. Robert Fulton's steamship was faster than any other riverboat at the time, and it could travel upstream almost as fast as it could travel downstream. As the steamboat carried people up and down the Hudson River between New York and Albany, it opened up the possibility of an easier way to travel deep into the American continent.

BEFORE ROBERT FULTON

The United States stretches 2,802 miles (4,509 km) from the Atlantic to the Pacific Ocean. Settlers, European explorers, and adventurers reached the continent on the eastern seaboard. To travel west, they had to cross mountains, forests, and prairies. There were no roads and few tracks. The easiest way to travel was by river.

MIGHTY RIVER

The Mississippi–Missouri is the longest river system in North America. It flows 3,902 miles (6,275 km) from the northwest of the United States, south to the Gulf of Mexico. The Ohio and many other rivers join the mighty Mississippi. Other rivers flow east, west, and south. For hundreds of years,

Before railroads were built, rivers provided ready-made routes across the land.

Native Americans traveled by river in canoes, and Europeans followed their example.

MAKING OF AMERICA

By the nineteenth century, Americans were farming the prairies, mining coal, and manufacturing goods. Louisville, Pittsburgh, and other towns developed as river ports, where goods were brought in and out by boat. Robert's steamship had led the way in establishing a river service. Lake and oceangoing steamships followed and helped make the United States a rich and powerful nation.

Robert's steamboat was faster and more reliable than other forms of river transport, making it possible to extend trade far inland.

Lewis and Clark

In 1804, two army officers, Meriwether Lewis and William Clark, paddled up the Missouri River from St. Louis to find the source of the river. They reached what is now Bismarck in North Dakota. From there, they climbed over the Rocky Mountains and traveled on west, down the Columbia River to the Pacific Ocean.

BEFORE STEAMBOATS

It is easier to haul goods along a river than to pull them across land. Floating downstream with the flow of the water is easy, but paddling upstream is hard work and slow. Sailboats do not work well on a river. There is often not enough room to maneuver and the wind is unreliable.

FLATBOATS AND KEELBOATS

Traders and settlers going west transported their possessions and goods along the Ohio River. Canoes were not large enough to carry goods, so people built flatboats, which were simply large, flat, wooden boxes used to transport things. Several men were needed to work the huge paddles of a flatboat, and when settlers arrived at their destination, many reused the wood of the boats to make houses. Keelboats had a pointed **bow** and were easier to steer than flatboats. However, passengers often had to help haul the boat by pulling it along with a rope.

STEAM ENGINES

Thomas Newcomen invented the first practical steam engine in 1712. Like an earlier engine invented by Thomas Savery, it was designed to drive a pump to remove water from

A flatboat was simple to construct and was large enough to carry all of a family's possessions, including any horses they may have owned.

mines and stop them from flooding. These early steam engines were large and heavy, and used huge amounts of coal. They could not be used in any form of transportation.

JAMES WATT'S IMPROVED ENGINE

In 1765, James Watt found a way to make the Newcomen engine more efficient. His engine made more power and used less fuel than Newcomen's. A steam engine works by heating water to make steam, which expands and moves a **piston**. In Newcomen's engines, the steam expanded and condensed in the same cylinder so that the engine constantly lost heat and power. Watt's engine solved this problem by having a separate condensing chamber.

James Watt's steam engine revolutionized steam power, but it was too huge to use for transportation. Watt was opposed to using steam engines in vehicles, because they were so dangerous.

The Word Is...

James Watt's steam engine was manufactured and sold by Matthew Boulton, an industrialist who was enthusiastic about the engine. He said:

"I sell here, Sir, what all the world desires to have, POWER."

WHO WAS ROBERT FULTON?

Robert was born on a farm in Little Britain (now called Fulton), near Lancaster, Pennsylvania, on November 14, 1765. He was born just six months after James Watt designed his improved steam engine. One of Watt's engines would power Robert to success almost 42 years later, but before that happened Robert was busy with other ideas and interests.

ROBERT'S CHILDHOOD

Robert's father had moved to Pennsylvania from Ireland and worked as a tailor as well as a farmer. His farm was not a success and was sold in 1771, when Robert was only five. The family then moved to Lancaster, where young Robert learned to read and write before going to school when he was eight. Lancaster was a center for people moving westward, and Robert learned about guns and wagons in the town's many workshops.

TALENT FOR PAINTING

Robert's first interest was painting, and he developed his skill by painting storefront and tavern signs. When he was about 15, he became an **apprentice** to a jeweler in Philadelphia. There, he became known for tiny portraits painted using just a single hair as a brush. These portraits were called miniatures and were used in lockets and pendants. By 1785, Robert had his own workshop and business as a miniature painter.

MOVE TO LONDON

Robert's paintings were so admired in Philadelphia that a group of local tradesmen gave him the money to travel to London to study painting with Benjamin West, a well-known American painter. Robert arrived in London in 1787 and stayed there for several years. Although his career as a painter was not a great success, he met many wealthy people who were interested in new ideas and inventions.

First Paddle boat

Robert's interest in **paddle boats** began early. When he was 13 years old, he fitted paddle wheels to a boat for his friends to paddle as they fished on the Conestoga Creek in Pennsylvania. He also made a rocket to celebrate Independence Day.

Robert's first paddle boat was powered by oars. As his friends rowed, the boat moved through the water, which turned the paddle wheels.

BUZZING WITH IDEAS

In the early 1790s, Robert moved from London to Devon, in England, to work with the Duke of Bridgewater and the Earl of Stanhope. These two wealthy men were his **patrons**, and they gave Robert money to develop his ideas. The duke and earl were both involved in inventions and canals, and this encouraged Robert to think about engineering, particularly canals and boats.

GRAND PLAN FOR CANALS

Robert saw how canals were more suitable than rivers for transporting people and goods, and wrote the *Treatise on the Improvement of Canal Navigation*, which was published in 1796. The plan included bridges, **aqueducts**, and one of Robert's inventions, a double-slope for lifting and lowering canal boats from one height of ground to another. Neither the double slope nor the plans were ever used.

A CET EMPLACEMENT DU QUAI DIT "DES BONSHO
L'INGENIEUR AMERICAIN ROBERT FULTO
PRESENTA LE 21 THERMIDOR DE L'AN XI (9 AOU
AUX CITOYENS
BOSSUT, CARNOT, PRONY ET VOLNEY
SON "CHARIOT D'EAU MÛ-PAR LE FEU"
QUI EFFECTUA SUR LA SEINE
SES PREMIERES EVOLUTIONS

A plaque on the bank of the Seine River in Paris, France, marks the place where Robert first tested his submarine, *Nautilus*.

AN INVENTIVE MIND

Robert knew that other American inventors were building boats driven by steam engines and he began to experiment with model boats. He found that a wheel of paddles at the **stern** of a boat was the best design for speed.

MOVE TO PARIS

In 1797, Robert moved to Paris. There, he invented a submarine for sinking enemy ships. His idea was that the boat would drop below the surface and force a large spike through the base of an enemy ship, before setting off a charge of gunpowder. He built the submarine, called the *Nautilus*, and tested it on the Seine River. These trials were successful, but when the *Nautilus* went into action, it was too slow to catch enemy ships.

This is a cutaway replica, or copy, of the *Nautilus*. It is kept at Cité de la Mer, Cherbourg, in France.

The Word Is...

Robert hoped that his inventions would make him wealthy. He had many disappointments and failures, but he did not give up. He said:

"The American dream of rags to riches is a dream for a reason, it is hard to achieve; were everyone to do it, it wouldn't be a dream but would rather be reality."

FIRST STEAMBOATS

While Robert was in Europe, inventors in the United States were figuring out ingenious ways of using a steam engine to power a boat. In 1787, both John Fitch and James Rumsey demonstrated steam-driven boats and then competed for the **patent**, which is the right to own an invention. As well as being scientists and engineers, inventors must have good business sense and be able to manage money and protect their invention from being copied.

A MECHANICAL CANOE

John Fitch's first steamboat had a row of paddles on each side of the boat, like paddles on a canoe, which pulled the boat through the water. In 1790, John launched an improved version of the ship and used it to run a regular service on the Delaware River from Philadelphia to Bordentown. Few people used the ferry, however, and John could not persuade any businessmen to back his steamboat. He even tried, unsuccessfully, to raise money to fund his invention in France.

WATER-JET ENGINE

Three months after John demonstrated his first steamboat, James Rumsey launched his steamboat on the Potomac River at Shepherdstown. It used a steam engine to pump water from the bow to the stern. It worked like a jet engine. As water was forced backward, the boat moved forward.

TWIN SCREWS

John Stevens was fascinated by John and James' steamships, and decided to build his own. He designed a **high-pressure** engine to deliver more power to the steamship, which he used to turn **propellers** instead of paddles. In 1798, his steamboat, the *Polacca*, traveled from Belleville in New Jersey to New York. The engine, however, caused such powerful vibrations that the ship was shaken apart!

Today, a road bridge crosses the Potomac River at Shepherdstown, where James Rumsey tested his water-jet steam engine. The bridge is named after the inventor.

Battle for Patent Rights

A patent is the legal right to an invention. That right means that someone else cannot copy the invention and make money from it. In John Fitch's and James Rumsey's time, each state granted its own patents, so both men were in a race to patent their inventions in different states.

ROBERT AND THE STEAMBOAT CHALLENGE

While Robert was in Paris, he was introduced to an American diplomat named Robert Livingston. This meeting, in 1801, would change Robert Fulton's life and the future of steamboats. Robert Livingston had acquired the **monopoly** for using steamboats in New York, which meant no one else could run steamboats there. His problem was that he did not have a working steamboat!

THE CHALLENGE

Robert Livingston's monopoly would last 20 years, but it had one condition: he had to build a steamboat that would travel no slower than 4 miles per hour (6.4 kph). When Robert Livingston heard about Robert Fulton's ideas for a steamship, the two formed a partnership. It was an exciting challenge and Robert Fulton began to build and test his designs.

Robert Livingston was a wealthy lawyer and one of the Founding Fathers. He joined forces with Robert Fulton to develop steamboat travel.

FIRST ATTEMPTS

Robert Fulton and Robert Livingston shared the cost of building the first boat, which was ready to test on the Seine River in 1803. It had a paddle wheel at one side of the stern, and used an engine designed by a French engineer. The engine, however, was too heavy for the **hull** of the boat, and it sank. Robert Fulton built a stronger hull, which worked better, but the boat was not fast enough.

RETURN TO NEW YORK

Robert Fulton then hit on the idea of using a James Watt engine, which was lighter but three times more powerful than any engine used in a boat. He ordered the engine from Boulton and Watt in England and asked for the parts to be sent to New York City. In 1806, Robert returned there, to receive and assemble the engine in 1807.

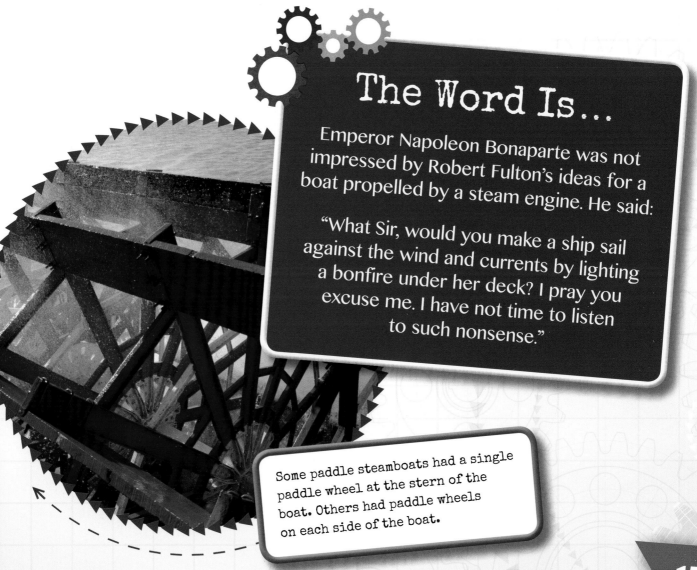

The Word Is...

Emperor Napoleon Bonaparte was not impressed by Robert Fulton's ideas for a boat propelled by a steam engine. He said:

"What Sir, would you make a ship sail against the wind and currents by lighting a bonfire under her deck? I pray you excuse me. I have not time to listen to such nonsense."

Some paddle steamboats had a single paddle wheel at the stern of the boat. Others had paddle wheels on each side of the boat.

BEATING THE RECORD

Robert lost no time in assembling Watt's engine and in overseeing the building of the boat at a shipyard on the East River. The boat was 130–140 feet (39–42.6 m) long, with two masts and a funnel. The steam engine drove a paddle wheel on each side of the boat. By August 17, 1807, the boat was ready to make its trial run from New York City, up the Hudson River to Albany, 150 miles (241 km) away.

The Hudson River winds through rugged countryside, mountains, and forests, just as it did in Robert's time.

STEAMING UPRIVER

A crowd of people gathered to watch the attempt in New York City. There were 140 people on board the boat, including Robert Fulton and Robert Livingston, but few expected the boat to move. At 1 p.m., Robert Fulton cast off and, with smoke and flames pouring from the funnel, the boat set off. Moments later, the engine stopped, but Robert adjusted it and the steamboat chugged upriver.

SUCCESS!

The boat reached Albany 32 hours later. It had traveled upstream, against the flow of the river, at an average speed of 4.7 miles per hour (7.6 kph). This was faster than the 4 miles per hour (6.4 kph) required for the monopoly, and much quicker than the four days it took a sailboat to make the same journey. Robert then returned to the starting point in New York City at about the same speed.

The Word Is...

This is part of a letter Robert wrote to a friend, describing the start of the historic voyage:

"My friends were in groups on the deck. There was anxiety mixed with fear among them. I read in their looks nothing but disaster, and almost repented my efforts. The signal was given and the boat moved on a short distance and then stopped . . . I could hear distinctly repeated 'I told you so; it is a foolish scheme.' When the boat started to move again, . . . all were still incredulous. None seemed willing to trust the evidence of their own senses."

This steamboat is a replica of Robert's victorious steamboat. He named it *Steamboat,* but it was later renamed the *Clermont.*

FIRST SERVICE

Robert's steamboat was faster than a sailboat, and it was reliable. The steam engine did not blow up, as many people expected, and the strength and direction of the wind did not affect its journey. By September 1807, Robert had started a regular ferry service making the round trip between New York City and Albany three times every two weeks. It was the first profitable steamboat service, and it opened the way for others.

THE *CLERMONT*

After its successful trial run, Robert made improvements to his steamboat, such as adding bunks to the cabins where passengers could comfortably sleep overnight. During the first winter, he strengthened and widened the hull. By 1808, the boat was 150 feet (45 m) long and the paddle wheels were 15 feet (4.5 m) in diameter. He renamed the boat the *New North River Steamboat of Clermont,* but it soon became known as the *Clermont.*

EXPANDING THE SERVICE

As soon as Robert Fulton and Robert Livingston began to make money from the steamboat service, they looked for ways to expand their business. They built more steamboats to run on the Hudson River and they looked for opportunities to start new steamboat ferries. Crossing a river is as important as traveling along it. Until the arrival of steamboats, crossings were made by horse-drawn ferries in New York, Philadelphia, and Boston. The ferries had flat bottoms and were rounded at each end, so that they could travel back and forth without needing to turn around. Fulton and Livingston's steamboats soon took over.

Robert's ferry service on the Hudson River took over much of the river trade. Smaller boats had to give way to the new steamboats.

At some river crossings, a ferry still carries people and vehicles across the river. This ferry is pulled from bank to bank by chains.

Setbacks

The *Clermont's* successful trial was not the end of Robert's problems. The boat developed various mechanical faults, which had to be fixed, and not everyone welcomed the new service. Robert took passengers and trade from sailboats that were already working on the Hudson River. The sailors tried to hinder the steamboat by "accidentally" sailing into it and damaging the paddle wheels. Robert boxed in the paddle wheels with wooden covers to protect them.

NAVIGATING THE MISSISSIPPI

Robert Fulton and Robert Livingston were eager to set up a steamboat ferry to link New Orleans on the Mississippi River with Pittsburgh on the Ohio River. First, Robert Livingston acquired a monopoly over steamboats on the lower Mississippi River, in the territory of New Orleans. Next, in 1810, Robert Fulton moved to Pittsburgh where he designed and built a steamboat to sail on the Mississippi River.

DOWNSTREAM FROM PITTSBURGH

On October 20, 1811, the *New Orleans* set off from Pittsburgh. The journey was 1,881 miles (3,027 km) long and difficult, with the bottom of the boat scraping sandbars on the riverbed. An earthquake even struck near Louisville during the journey! Nevertheless, the *New Orleans* successfully completed the trip, arriving in New Orleans on January 12, 1812.

THE RETURN JOURNEY

When the boat started the journey upstream, the engine was not powerful enough to take the ship against the strong current farther than Natchez, Mississippi. Robert Fulton built three more boats in New Orleans but none reached more than 3 miles per hour (4.8 kph) upstream, and none made it to Pittsburgh. Instead, for the next two years, Robert Fulton and Robert Livingston ran a ferry service between New Orleans and Natchez.

FINAL YEARS

Robert Fulton continued to pursue other ideas, including his submarine and an armed warship, which he tried to sell to the government. He spent a lot of time and money fighting legal challenges to his monopolies and patents. He died unexpectedly after an accident on the frozen Hudson River. When a friend fell through the ice, Robert rescued him from the icy water, but caught pneumonia as a result and died on February 24, 1815.

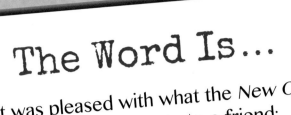

The Word Is...

Robert was pleased with what the *New Orleans* achieved. He wrote to a friend:

"The Mississippi . . . is conquered; the steamboat, which I have sent to trade between New Orleans and Natchez, carried 1,500 barrels, equal to 150 tons, . . . against the current, 313 miles in seven days, working in that time 84 hours."

The Erie Canal links the Hudson River with Lake Erie. Robert was excited by the canal's potential, but he died before it was completed.

OPENING UP AMERICA

The *New Orleans* had shown that the Mississippi River could be **navigated** and others quickly took up the challenge. At first, they were hindered by Robert Livingston's monopoly of the lower Mississippi, until a court overturned it in 1815. The decision opened the way for Henry Miller Shreve to make the first steamboat voyage from New Orleans to Louisville.

SUCCESS OF THE *WASHINGTON*

Henry learned the lessons of Robert Fulton's failure. His steamboat, the *Washington*, had a shallower hull and a lighter, more powerful engine. In September 1816, the ship reached Louisville on the Ohio River from New Orleans. The following year, it made the round trip between the two cities in just 41 days.

MISSISSIPPI STEAMBOATS

Faster steamboats followed, with captains racing each other. The boats carried cotton and sugar from plantations to

Vicksburg Landing, on the Mississippi River, became a busy port. Even in 1905, cargo and passengers were being loaded and unloaded from steamboats there.

New Orleans, and they also carried passengers. Large steamboats, furnished in the style of expensive hotels, offered passengers a taste of luxury.

EXPANDING SERVICE

As Henry's design was improved, steamboats shortened the journey time between New Orleans and Louisville from Henry's 25 days to 4.5 days. Ferry services expanded, bringing trade, jobs, and creating new towns along the Great Lakes and the Ohio-Mississippi and Missouri rivers into Montana. The Columbia and Colorado rivers carried the trade to the Pacific Ocean. Rivers remained the main means of transportation in the United States until steam locomotives and the railroads took over in the 1870s.

The *Robert E. Lee* steamboat is best known for beating the *Natchez*, which had been the fastest steamboat, in a race from New Orleans to St. Louis in 1870.

The Word Is...

Mark Twain (born Samuel Clemens) grew up near Hannibal on the banks of the Mississippi River. He wrote:

"When I was a boy, there was but one permanent ambition among my comrades in our village on the west bank of the Mississippi River. That was, to be a steamboatman."

Clemens was a steamboat pilot for four years and later took the name Mark Twain. It means "two fathoms" or 12 feet (3.6 m) of water, the safe depth for a Mississippi steamboat.

STEAMING ACROSS THE OCEAN

Until 1809, most people believed that steamboats could not survive the rough waters of the oceans, but John Stevens and his son Robert proved them wrong when their steamboat the *Phoenix* made the first ocean journey from Perth Amboy in New Jersey to Delaware Bay in Philadelphia. They had to make the voyage by ocean because Robert Livingston's monopoly prevented John from using his boats on New York rivers.

EASTERN SEABOARD

It took the *Phoenix* 13 days to complete the 150-mile (241 km) journey to Delaware Bay. There, the Stevens family ran a successful steamboat service on the Delaware River between Philadelphia and Trenton. Nevertheless, other steamships followed the *Phoenix's* example and began to carry passengers and goods along the east coast to South Carolina and Georgia.

FIRST ATLANTIC CROSSING

Steamships kept close to the coast until 1819, when the *Savannah* left New York City and sailed across the Atlantic Ocean. It arrived in Liverpool on the west coast of England on July 20, 27 days and 11 hours after leaving New York City. The ship carried sails and used the steam engine for only 85 hours during the journey. It later returned to the United States by sail.

THE BREAKTHROUGH

The main problem for steamships on long voyages was that the huge amounts of coal they had to carry left no room for cargo. British engineer Isambard Kingdom Brunel solved the problem by strengthening the wooden hulls of steamships with iron, which allowed him to build bigger, stronger ships. The *Great Western* began a regular transatlantic service between Bristol and New York City in 1838.

The Great Eastern

In 1858, Isambard Brunel launched the *Great Eastern*. It was the biggest ship of the time at 692 feet (211 m) long, and carried 4,000 passengers. The ship had an iron hull, paddle wheels, and a screw propeller. It had five funnels, four for the engines that drove the paddle wheels, and one for the propeller's engine. The ship also carried sails.

The *Great Eastern* held the record as the biggest ship for more than 40 years, but was not a great commercial success.

THE END OF STEAMBOATS

Robert Fulton's *Clermont*, the first successful steamboat ferry, forged the way for steamboat services on American inland waterways. However, by the 1860s, riverboats had given way to railroads, and steamboats became mainly a tourist attraction. The heyday for ocean steamships had only just begun and continued until the middle of the twentieth century.

GOLDEN AGE OF STEAMSHIPS

By the end of the nineteenth century, steamships were benefitting from improved engineering, particularly **steam turbine** engines and **twin screw propellers**. Steamships became bigger and faster. Companies competed by offering faster journeys in luxury cabins to wealthy passengers crossing the Atlantic, at the same time as accommodating poor emigrants from Europe in less comfortable third class cabins, or "steerage."

THE END OF THE LINE

The days of the huge liners driven by steam engines came to an end soon after World War II (1939–1945).

In 1906, the *Lusitania* was the largest, fastest, and one of the most luxurious steamships to sail across the Atlantic Ocean.

First, **diesel** engines replaced steam engines but passenger ships were unable to compete with aircraft, which reduced a sea journey of a week to a flight measured in hours. Today, large ships are used as cruise liners, or to carry oil and cargo across the world.

WILL STEAM MAKE A COMEBACK?

Steam power is generated by heating water to make steam. Traditionally, this was mostly done by burning coal, which we now know causes dangerous amounts of pollution. However, if steam could be made without burning fossil fuels, it could be used again. Some engineers are already working on modern steam-driven cars!

Problem with Coal

Coal is bulky and dirty. Oil and natural gas provide more energy than the same weight of coal and create less pollution. However, all fossil fuels pollute the air when they are burned. They produce large amounts of carbon dioxide and other gases that trap the sun's heat, making Earth warmer. In the past, higher temperatures have changed habitats, making millions of species extinct. Engineers must find good alternatives to fossil fuels, and quickly!

TIMELINE

1712 Thomas Newcomen invents the first practical steam engine.

1765 James Watt invents a more efficient steam engine than Newcomen's. Robert Fulton is born in Little Britain near Lancaster, Pennsylvania, on November 14.

Robert Fulton worked in Britain, France, and America, transforming both river and ocean transportation.

1771 The Fulton family move to Lancaster.

1780–87 Robert works as an apprentice and becomes a miniature-portrait painter.

1787 Robert moves to London, England, to work for painter Benjamin West. John Fitch and James Rumsey demonstrate steam-driven boats.

1790 John Fitch sets up a regular ferry service on the Delaware River, using an improved steamboat.

1790s Robert moves to Devon, where he becomes interested in canals and engineering.

1796 Robert's *Treatise on the Improvement of Canal Navigation* is published.

1797 Robert moves to Paris, France.

1798 John Stevens's propeller-driven steamboat, the *Polacca*, travels from Belleville, New Jersey, to New York City.

1800 Robert builds the *Nautilus*, a submarine powered by hand.

1801 Robert Fulton meets Robert Livingston in Paris, France.

1803 Robert Fulton and Robert Livingston test their first steamboat on the Seine River.

1806 Robert returns to New York City.

1807 August 17–18, Robert's steamship makes its successful test run on the Hudson River. Robert begins a regular ferry service between New York City and Albany.

1808 Robert Fulton and Harriet Livingston, John Livingston's niece, marry. John Livingston acquires a monopoly over steamboats on the Mississippi River in the territory of New Orleans.

1809 The first ocean voyage is made by John Stevens' steamboat, the *Phoenix*, from Perth Amboy, New Jersey, to Delaware Bay.

1810 Robert moves to Pittsburgh.

1811 Robert's steamboat the *New Orleans* sets off on October 20 along the Ohio River.

1812 The *New Orleans* reaches New Orleans on January 12. Robert is appointed a member of the commission that recommends that the Erie Canal is built. Robert builds the first steam warship to protect New York City from the British.

This replica of the *North River Steamboat* (*Clermont*), Robert's first steamship, was launched in 1909 on the Hudson River.

1813 Robert Livingston dies on February 26.

1815 Robert Fulton dies on February 24. Robert Livingston's monopoly on the lower Mississippi River is overturned by a court decision.

1816 Henry Miller Shreve's steamboat the *Washington* travels upstream from New Orleans and reaches Louisville.

1819 The *Savannah* makes the first crossing of the Atlantic Ocean using a steam engine for part of the way.

1838 The *Great Western* begins a regular passenger service across the Atlantic between New York City and Bristol, in England.

1858 The *Great Eastern* is launched.

GLOSSARY

apprentice A person who learns a skill by working with an expert.

aqueducts Bridges that carry water across valleys.

bow The front of a boat.

diesel A type of heavy oil, used mainly in engines that power large vehicles such as locomotives and ships.

high-pressure Producing a strong force by squeezing a gas or liquid.

hull The body of a boat.

monopoly The legal right to be the only person or company that can own or sell a particular product.

navigated Followed a path from one place to another.

paddle boats Boats that are driven by paddles, usually arranged into one or two wheels that push backward through the water as they turn, moving the boats forward.

patent The legal right to own an invention.

patrons People who help an artist or businessperson by giving them money and encouragement.

piston A solid, movable cylinder that fits inside a hollow cylinder.

propellers Machines for producing movement in a ship or aircraft. A propeller has sloping blades attached to a rod. As the rod turns, the blades twist or screw through the water or air.

steam turbine An engine that uses the force of steam to turn a shaft or rod.

stern The back of a boat.

twin screw propellers Two propellers that work in different directions to keep a boat moving steadily forward.

Books

Aramini, Jamie. *Munford Meets Robert Fulton* (The Adventures of Munford). Nancy, KY: Geography Matters, 2011.

Herweck, Don. *Making It Go: The Life and Work of Robert Fulton* (Science Readers). Huntington Beach, CA: Teacher Created Materials Publishing, 2007.

Herweck, Don. *Robert Fulton: Engineer of the Steamboat* (Mission: Science Biographies). North Mankato, MN: Compass Point Books, 2008.

Rebman, Renée C. *Robert Fulton's Steamboat* (We the People). Mankato, MN: Compass Point Books, 2007.

Roberts, Steven. *Robert Fulton* (Jr. Graphic American Inventors). New York, NY: PowerKids Press, 2013.

Sich, Jenny. *100 Inventions That Made History.* New York, NY: DK Publishing, 2014.

Websites

Due to the changing nature of Internet links, PowerKids Press has developed an online list of websites related to the subject of this book. This site is updated regularly. Please use this link to access the list: **www.powerkidslinks.com/itctw/fulton**

INDEX